RETURN
FROM
NOWHERE

A *family memoir*

JULIAN BRONHOLC

NEWMAN SPRINGS PUBLISHING
320 Broad Street
Red Bank, NJ 07701

First originally published by Newman Springs Publishing 2023

ISBN 979-8-89061-282-3 (Paperback)
ISBN 979-8-89061-283-0 (Digital)

Printed in the United States of America

In memory of my late wife, Pnina Bronholc,
who was my wife for sixty years.
In memory of my late parents, Hana
Myshkin and Berko Bronholc.

PROLOGUE

It took quite some time for me to reach the determination to put in writing the events that were horrendous in nature but, in actuality, saved my life. It appears that cataclysmic events tend to suppress or invoke memories during childhood.

Some of the events from when I was three to four years old are still vivid in my memory. The nagging question as to why I was one of the few Jews to remain alive while six million perished will probably never be answered.

With the passage of time, this question instilled in me a feeling of responsibility to share my early life history with my children and colleagues. Many who have heard my survival story continued to urge me to preserve it for the present and future generations.

My miraculous survival of the worst period in Jewish history is the main reason to share and record my early life history. Survival of cataclysmal events is a combination of luck, circumstances, and genetic prowess given by nature.

The events described took place between 1939 and 1946 in a locale which extends from the town of Suwałki in northeastern Poland to the Beregayevo Gulag deep in Russian Siberia. It encompasses a return trek in cattle cars via Kyrgyzstan to the southwestern part of postwar Poland which was annexed from Germany.

The following story will tell what spared me from becoming human ash or a piece of human soap made from dead Jews by the Germans.

One of the most memorable events took place after our resettlement in western Poland. One day, after returning home from grammar school, I found my stepmother Rivka deep in tears, shocked and extremely agitated. Her face was reddish, tears were rolling down her cheeks, and her hand pointed to a bar of soap lying on the kitchen table. It took me a while to get the entire story from her. The soap in the house that was assigned to us by Polish authorities was made in concentration camps from the bodies of slaughtered Jews.

This shocking experience was also one of the reasons to tell my survival story. To this very day, a jar containing soap made from the bodies of dead Jews is stored with other trial documents in the archive of the international court in Hague.

The jars with human soap were evidence of the atrocities presented during the Nuremberg trials. There were other products made from dead Jews by the Nazis. One such item was a lampshade made from the skin of Holocaust victims which was priced online for $26,800 in Romania. The Romanian government stopped this despicable, outrageous, and macabre trade.

All events described in this memoir were given to me by my brother, Eli; my father, Berko; and my stepmother, Rivka, or recorded in my memory.

MY BIRTHPLACE

I was born on July 8, 1937, to Berko Bronholc and Hana Myshkin Bronholc in the town of Suwałki. Suwałki is located in the northeastern corner of Poland.

Suwałki borders Russia and Lithuania. Being a border town, Suwałki became involved in the Napoleonic Wars and subsequently in World War I and World War II.

Suwałki is the coldest spot in all of Poland, known for freezing winters and hot summers. The variety of flora and fauna made this town famous as a playground for the richest in Europe. The immense forests and lakes attracted scores of well-to-do Europeans.

Being the second child, I became the object of envy of my older brother, Elkana. It took some years for me to note his consequential behavior toward me which included elements of jealousy, and, being the youngest in the family, attracting the love and attention of my loving parents.

Suwałki, a pastoral small town, was a place of harmonious coexistence between approximately eleven thousand Jews and other ethnic groups including Poles, Russians, Romas, and Lithuanians.

The community of Suwałki received prominence from a number of inhabitants who lived and thrived in the city's boundaries. These notable people were Zalman Gradowski, a secret diarist of Auschwitz-Birkenau; Josef Hassid, a violinist; Maria Konopnicka, a poet, novelist, and writer for children; Mieczysław Mackiewicz, a general of the Polish army who was killed in the Katyn massacre; Aleksandra Piłsudski, wife of Jozef Piłsudski and Polish First Lady; Abraham Stern, a Jewish parliamentary leader who founded and led Lehi (the Stern Gang); and Andrzej Wajda, a film director.

Suwałki also became known as a cradle of Jewish philanthropy and social support in all facets of communal living.

The town of Suwałki enjoyed free and compulsory elementary education, but the parents preferred to send their children to Talmud Torah and Tarbut schools, which required certain fees.

The town of Suwałki had a Jewish community board in charge of maintenance of religious institutions, appointments of rabbis, rituals of slaughter, ritual baths, and managing burials. It also supported religious and vocational schools, Jewish hospitals, and charity institutions as well as orphanages.

The city also had an old-age home, interest-free loan institutions, assistance for families of fallen soldiers, assistance in the supplying of wood and fuel, and the distribution of bread and potatoes for the poor. There were also city organizations which helped people get married and supplied clothing. The city of Suwałki became an early model of community support for all Jewish diaspora throughout Europe and later the American continents.

My father, Berko, grew up without parents as they died during his early childhood. He was helped by his grandmother who took care of him with her meager means. The need to survive from a young age forced him to engage in street sales in which he became very successful.

The affinity for street sales brought my father to Argentina, known at the time as a haven for street peddlers. He was very successful overseas, but his love for my mother, Hana, brought him back to Suwałki, where he became the owner of a grocery store. My mother joined my father in running the grocery store.

The store became known as well-supplied, giving customers credit for those unable to pay immediately. His name became famous in town for his generosity and his help to people in need. Suffering hunger at a young age made my father compassionate toward those less fortunate. I was often taken to the store and placed on an elevated shelf, easily able to observe both my parents serving their customers.

My father had a personal friend who was an international salesman. This friend traveled throughout Europe most of the time. This salesman enjoyed the full trust of my father.

By nature, my father was very hard-headed, but there was no family member or acquaintance who could persuade him more than this friend. My father had a deep trust in this man and unquestioningly followed his advice.

One day, upon returning from a sales trip in Germany, this friend told my father that the Germans, under the command of Adolf Hitler, would soon be invading Poland and killing every Jew. My father took this warning seriously and decided to leave his home and business with his family in tow. He crossed the Russian border illegally, leaving everything behind. We were a family of four moving into the unknown world.

I vaguely remember sitting alone on the horse carriage between sacks of products, bed covers, and pillows. The rest of my family, following the carriage, traveled by foot. This also included the owner of the horse. I recall my mother crying silently.

Later on, I was told that my mother did not want to leave our house and store, but she had to follow the strong will of my father. She was strongly connected to the Jewish community of Suwałki. It appears that she had a premonition that she would never return back to Suwałki's Jewish life.

OUTBREAK OF THE SECOND WORLD WAR AND THE ANNIHILATION OF JEWS IN SUWAŁKI

The Second World War broke out on Friday, September 1, 1939. I was a two-year-old child of a happy, prosperous family. German forces still had not entered Suwałki several days after the outbreak of the war. They were content with heavy bombing.

My father, remembering what his traveling salesman friend told him about Hitler's intention of killing all the Jews, hired a horse and cart, put me in it with some provisions and belongings, and moved southeast toward the Russian border.

Since the Germans were already very close by, my father had to look for safe roads, and we traveled mostly at night. We finally reached a town named Sokółka, disposed of the horse and cart, and embarked by train. The railway station underwent extremely heavy bombing. While on the moving train car, I was held in my mother's arms.

Despite heavy fire from the German planes, I remember screaming the Yiddish word, "*Lekach! Lekach!*" This is a word for a type of cake made with flour mixed with eggs and honey. While most of the passengers in the railcar were thirsty and hungry, my screams demanding a Jewish pastry caused rather large consternation for my family. This forced my brother Elkana to silence me with blows to the head.

We had been bombed and machine-gunned once more by German planes and finally reached the town of Baranowicze, which was our final destination.

In the wake of another bombing attack, we left Baranowicze for a village near the Soviet border which we stayed in until the arrival of the Red Army. After several days, we returned to Baranowicze.

A few days later, my father heard that according to the Molotov-Ribbentrop Pact, an agreement was reached wherein the Russian Army was going to leave, and the Germans were taking over the town.

My father rented another horse and cart, loaded provisions and other merchandise from the store in Suwałki, and brought them to a city named Brest-Litovsk where we had a family. We lived there for some time but, as refugees, were commanded to leave for another place at a distance of at least one hundred kilometers from the newly established Soviet border on the Bug River. Thus, we reached the town of Kovel.

After the immediate outbreak of World War II, the city of Suwałki, much to the surprise of the remaining Jews, was occupied by the Red Army and not by the Germans. This fact caused immense joy among the Jewish population who welcomed the entry of the Red Army into town. This joyful situation did not last long. After one week, the Soviet soldiers left Suwałki.

My father became seriously troubled when he heard that the Soviets left Suwałki. All his possessions, including the house, the store, and other assets were left under German control. After the short presence of the Red Army, the Germans gained control of Suwałki with disastrous results. The entry of Germans into Suwałki brought about apocalyptic results for the Jewish presence. Despite a strong belief within the Jewish community that war would not break out, the German soldiers entered Suwałki during the second week of September 1939.

During the second day of the war, a large bombardment occurred in Suwałki without the presence of German soldiers on the ground. Although Poland was invaded on September 1, 1939, no German boots were on the ground in Suwałki. Many young Jews were conscripted into the Polish army despite the sheer despair of their families still remembering the first world war.

There were instances of antisemitic hooliganism against Suwałki Jews. Local populations came from other towns to attack the Jews still living in Suwałki. In addition to the impending German invasion, the Jewish population of Suwałki had to fend off cases of upcoming pogroms from the dwellers of surrounding towns.

There was a need to mobilize monetary resources so that local Suwałki hooligans would protect against outside antisemites from the surrounding towns. Jewish guards had to patrol Jewish neighborhoods, orphanages, old-age homes, synagogues, hospitals, and the Jewish cemetery. On the morning of Simchat Torah, it became evident that the Russian army left Suwałki and that the German soldiers had taken possession of the town. There were rumors that Jews were being beaten in the streets by German soldiers, that Jewish shops were robbed, and that men of any age were taken by force for labor.

The established head officer of the Gestapo informed the Jewish leaders about the need to vacate the town within three days. The synagogues were shut down, and the keys were taken away by the Germans. After pleading from the rabbi, the expulsion of Jews was extended to fourteen days.

The frantic Jews, including the rabbi and his family, tried to cross the border into Lithuania or Russia, but all of them were closed and heavily patrolled by the local police and border soldiers. Thousands of Jews found themselves in the forests, trying to cross the borders. They were forced to go back. The family of the rabbi sustained casualties when the border police opened fire on the family while trying to cross the border. The daughter of the rabbi was one of the casualties. Doom and gloom fell upon the Jewish community of Suwałki.

None of the surrounding towns in Lithuania or Russia allowed the Suwałki Jews to enter. Jews were huddled in forests, exposed to cold nights in the open. The two-week extension was running out for the Jews who were to leave Suwałki, even though they were forbidden to cross the border into Lithuania. Very few Jews were able to cross the border illegally into Lithuania.

The Jews that remained in Suwałki after the expiration period to vacate the town were herded into cattle cars and transported to the Lublin area's concentration camps. All of them were killed shortly after arrival. The remaining Jews in Suwałki were taken into the surrounding forests by the Einsatzgruppen and shot. The Jews who were successful in crossing the border into Lithuania or Russia were killed when Russia was invaded on June 22, 1941, by Hitler's army. No single living Jew remained in Suwałki. The entire Jewish community had been totally exterminated. The providentially inspired decision of my father to not accept Russian citizenship saved our lives, but the penalty was being sent to Siberia.

SEEKING REFUGE
IN RUSSIA

The outbreak of World War II brought my family to the town of Kovel in eastern Russia. Russian authorities interrogated the head of every family which arrived.

According to the highly suspicious Russian authorities, the illegal crossing of a foreign population could bring potential spies to the border towns. Lacking evidence of hostile intentions from my father, the Russian secret service offered him Russian citizenship. My father, as well as a few other Jews, refused to accept the offer of citizenship. My father's refusal landed my entire family on an

NKVD list (later KGB). This was known as the Siberian list.

After the invasion of Russia into Poland on September 17, 1939, the list grew to about eight hundred thousand Polish intellectuals, clergy members, military officers, and government members. All were exiled to Siberia.

Filmmaker Steven Spielberg created a famous movie entitled *Schindler's List*. This movie depicted approximately one thousand Jewish laborers in concentration camps who were employed by German entrepreneur and Nazi sympathizer Oskar Schindler. These laborers made pots and uniforms for the German army. They were in a concentration camp named Płaszów not far from Krakow. They were more witnesses to the Holocaust rather than actual victims.

To a certain degree, these prisoners were more protected by Oskar Schindler than any other camp prisoners or detainees in Russian gulags. He was in charge of making sure that they received adequate food and, if needed, medical care. I strongly hope that the memory of the eight hundred thousand detainees will be part of a movie like *Schindler's List*, possibly a movie named *Siberian List*.

We were arrested one night by the NKVD and put in cattle cars as a result of my father's refusal to accept Russian citizenship. After a two-month journey (escorted by NKVD forces), we reached a Siberian taiga station deep in Siberia (the town of Asino).

From there, all deportees embarked on a steamboat, and after three days' worth of sailing on the Chulym River (a supply artery of the Ob River), we disembarked at a village named Bieregayevo. The year was 1940. From there, we were brought to the final destination of deportation via a narrow rail train. It was a gulag camp cleared of almost all previous political prisoners. The majority of Jewish refugees who frightfully accepted Russian citizenship were allowed to stay in the Russian border towns.

As mentioned earlier, following Hitler's 1939 invasion of Poland, all the remaining Jews in Suwałki were shot in the surrounding forests by SS units. Following Hitler's invasion of Russia in 1941 (Operation Barbarossa), all Jewish refugees who accepted Russian citizenship and remained in the border towns were exterminated by special units of the so-called SS *Einsatzgruppen*. There were four groups acting in different parts of Russia, all under well-educated German commanders.

Part of the Jewish population living in the Ukrainian territory was killed by local Ukrainians. They allowed the German soldiers to act as spectators during this decimation. Thousands of Jewish men, women, and children were killed by Ukrainians in the streets of many towns. The bloodshed of Jewish victims became a daily occurrence. Ukrainian women, dressed in holiday garb, met the incoming German soldiers with plates of bread and sweets. The Ukrainian population welcomed the invading Germans as liberators. They were seen as heroes who were setting the local population free from communist oppression.

The memory of approximately five million dispossessed Ukrainian landowners being sent to perish in gulags by Stalin was still very vivid and alive. My father's providentially guided decision to refuse Russian citizenship saved our lives at the outbreak of the war. We were now facing the task of surviving the hellish conditions in Siberia.

The first two words in Russian that were the daily welcoming slogan by the gulag guards were "*oprivikhiesh o'zdochniesh*," which literally meant, "Either you will get used to such life, or you will perish." These were the first words I learned in Russian, and I will never forget them for the rest of my life.

LIFE IN THE GULAG

Siberia is one of the largest parts of the Russian Federation.

It is the most desolate and one of the most mineral-rich parts of the globe. It is known for its extreme continentally cold climate and vast permafrost expanses. The gulag was a collection of simple wooden barracks without electricity, heat, or running water. There were no fences around the compound.

Prisoners could not survive or reach a sustainable place in case of attempted escape. Subzero temperatures do not leave room for survival. Life in the depths of the Siberian wilderness (locally called Beregayevo) beyond the Ob River was typically the site of the

Russian gulag. Subfreezing temperatures of negative 65 degrees Celsius, combined with the absence of electricity, heat, running water, and scarce food (with rapid outbreaks of typhoid and lice infestations) decimated the detained population. The survival rate was less than 10 percent.

My brother, Elkana, and I survived bouts of malaria without medication.

I was unaware that my father smuggled a few kilograms of gold coins for a rainy day. Only he and my mother were privy to this information. One night, our room was invaded by an NKVD squad (secret police). They wore intimidating uniforms and brandished guns and flashlights. I was put by one of these raiders on an elevated wooden plank. I was able to see the entire area from my perch. Using bayonets and knives, they ripped pillows and bed covers apart. The room quickly filled with white snow-like feathers.

After a short while, I heard metal coins hitting the permafrost floor. The sound of these falling coins persisted for a long time. These gold coins were collected by the NKVD crew and confiscated for the Russian war effort. Any attempt to regain this fortune during and after the war was fruitless.

The only outcome of this raid was the arrest of my father for owning foreign currency during a time of war. My mother's command of the Russian language helped my father to land quite a lucrative job as the manager of all the supply accommodations for the camp. My mother had to assist my father in his daily work, so my brother was assigned to take care of me. Some of the most memorable events from this time period were the fishing trips my brother and I took in a canoe carved from a tree trunk.

I was required to sit still to prevent the flipping of the canoe. Sitting for long hours motionless made me frantic with fear of drowning in the lake. I must admit that my brother was a very strict person of a pedantic nature. He also possessed despotic inclinations. He was very inventive during the harshest time that my family experienced. From scratch, he was able to manufacture the basic tools needed for survival. All the fishing equipment (sinkers, floats, and hooks) were manufactured and adjusted by him to ensure survival.

Elkana demanded from others what he demanded from himself. He was very composed and in control of any situation that arose. He knew how to produce to survive, but there was no compassion in his behavior during these trying times. Many times, he whipped me with birch twigs for the smallest of transgressions or not fulfilling his orders to his satisfaction.

Taking a shower in the gulag became one of the most important events. Because of the lack of partitions, the women hung blankets to separate the shower area from the living area. A small group of children aged three to four (including myself) were left alone to see the spectacle of communal showers taken by naked women. Despite my young age, those showers were major events.

On June 22, 1941, Hitler's army attacked Russia. Russia sustained enormous losses in manpower and equipment. The splitting of Polish territories between the Germans and the Russians after the Molotov-Ribbentrop Pact brought many Polish citizens under Russian control. The Russian secret police forced many Polish citizens into exile in Siberia. About eight hundred thousand

Polish citizens (including Jews) were forced into Russian gulags in Siberia.

Because of the catastrophic situation of the Russian armed forces, an agreement was reached between Stalin and General Sikorski on July 30, 1941. This agreement granted amnesty to Polish citizens exiled to the Soviet Union by the Russian secret police in 1940 and 1941. The conditions for the granting of this amnesty included a promise that all young Poles would be mobilized in the war effort to help the badly defeated Russian armed forces.

This agreement freed us from the Siberian gulag.

Later in life, my father told me about the prominence of Naftali Frenkel, a Jewish prisoner in the gulag who received fame for transforming gulag prisons into successful business enterprises for the communist Russian regime. He was also arrested for illegally crossing the Russian border. While a prisoner in the gulag, he invented the idea of matching food rations for prisoners with their rate of work production. This contributed to the demise of many prisoners (starvation) by helping the stronger ones survive.

He became a favorite of Stalin at the expense of thousands of suffering gulag prisoners who perished in Siberia. His business methods in the gulags brought on a new dimension of hatred toward the Jewish people. He also became a gulag advisor to other communist Jewish leaders such as Yagoda and Kaganovich. The case of Naftali Frenkel was an example of the source of historical hatred toward the Jewish people based on the activity of an absolute minority of Jewish activists (those who joined the revolutionary movement).

Throughout history, the majority of Jews suffered for the involvement of an absolute minority of Jews in radical movements such as the Russian Revolution. The enemies of the Jewish race used this constantly as a pretext to punish and terrorize the Jewish population across Europe. The majority of the Jewish population was doomed to pay an undeserved penalty for zealotry and the involvement and support of revolutionary activities undertaken by *very few* Jews.

FAREWELL TO SIBERIA

The agreement between Stalin and General Sikorski enabled the exiled Polish government to set all Polish dwellers of the gulag free. This allowed them to embark on a journey all the way back from Siberia and Asia Minor toward the Iranian border to leave the Soviet Union.

The Sikorski-Mayski agreement was signed on July 30, 1941. This agreement granted amnesty to the exiled Polish citizens who were exiled to Siberia after the Soviet takeover of Polish territories in 1939.

The demarcation line was designated at the Bug River. *Amnesty* was the wrong word to use because, in fact, none of the resettled inhabitants who went to Siberia were ever convicted.

One of the requirements of the agreement was that the Polish army would be established on Soviet soil or be sent elsewhere. This agreement provided the opportunity for Polish citizens in Siberia to volunteer for the Polish army.

This news spread very slowly, and it created a lot of misinformation and delays while the war was still raging in Europe. Many deportees were confused with the dilemma of traveling into unknown territory or remaining in place until the situation cleared up. They were also unsure if they should plan their own departure or wait until the Russian administration organized transportation.

This situation caused a split in families who had sick family members who had to stay in place while the rest of the family left. There was an urgent need to use self-made rafts on rivers leading to the nearest railway stations. The entire gulag population had to move from the extreme cold to the warmer southern part of the Asian continent. The army being formed was under the command of General Władysław Anders.

Red aster flowers growing on the hills of Monte Cassino in Italy became a symbol of Polish soldiers' heroism and bloodshed during an attempt to dislodge the German invasion during World War II.

The Polish soldiers, freed from Russian gulags, were assigned to the battle at Monte Cassino. Participation in this battle against Hitler's aggression was the primary reason the Polish detainees were freed from the camps by the Soviets.

They were put under the command of General Władysław Anders.

The sheer, unlimited heroism of these Polish soldiers became a permanent record in the annals of human bravery and sacrifice and exemplified the strive for freedom for their country and all of mankind

This was Poland's contribution to the entire world. These Polish prisoners were given freedom to fight for their country while setting an example for future generations.

The journey south became a lasting nightmare. Trains heading south were exceedingly scarce. The existing railway system was overloaded with trains headed in different directions. Some were moving the Red Army westward while others relocated factories and workers to the east.

There was a tremendous flow of Polish citizens from the north to the south. Food and water were rare commodities. Many families became separated while searching for food or water when the trains stopped suddenly. There was no information available as to when the trains would start moving again.

Hot water was referred to as *kipiatok*, and it was in high demand. My family became separated at least half a dozen times because my father would venture for food and water every time the train stopped. It was a harrowing experience for me to lose my father, not knowing if I would ever see him again. As a four-year-old, I was constantly scared and worried that I would permanently lose my father.

I must admit that my father had the uncanny ability to find our train on his own after disappearing in a completely different location. It required a lot of courage and skill to reach departed trains at different stations under these tumultuous conditions.

Many people succumbed to disease and starvation during the journey south. There was not enough food, and many evacuees were sent to a kolkhoz, a communal enterprise where irrigation ditches were dug or cotton was picked for meager rations of food.

The conditions experienced on the trip southward were worse than the experience of living in a gulag. Several thousand transportees died along the way from dysentery. The most vulnerable were small children and the elderly. There was no medical help or drugs to alleviate the outburst of dysentery or typhoid epidemics.

This nightmarish journey from the gulag was an "every man for himself" battle where only the strongest survived the ordeal. It is hard to comprehend my survival during this period.

Despite my physical survival, my childhood continued to be destroyed. There were so many more *stations* in my life that had to be crossed without being critically hurt. The journey from the gulag to Kyrgyzstan was a harrowing experience where only the fittest survived.

LIFE IN
KYRGYZSTAN

Because of the continuous war in Europe, we were forced to settle in the Republic of Kyrgyzstan, and we remained there for the next five years.

My father was arrested twice for attempting to sell goods and products without a proper license. My entire family was sickened with typhoid. My father, my brother, and I survived. My mother passed away. I lost my mother at the age of four. My memories from this timeframe are foggy because of my age.

I remember the day when my father came home from the hospital after the death of my mother. He was hitting his forehead with his hands in despair and screaming that "Chana is not anymore, and that she will never come home again." My father was extremely emotional during this ordeal.

As a child, the unexpected loss of my mother created a feeling of emptiness and placed me in a state of constant fear of the unknown. I was sleepless for many nights, hoping that somehow my mother would show herself again.

After my mother's death, my father was taken to a Russian labor camp. I and my brother were left alone. I was afraid to be alone after my mother's death. This fear continued for a very long time. I ventured outside at the age of five, looking for the company of older people. I wanted to pretend that they were relatives or acquaintances.

Walking with strangers became the norm. It gave me a feeling of security and possible protection in case of danger. For some unknown reason, I felt compelled to join any funeral procession, walking close to the open casket, and watching if the deceased would miraculously open their eyes with renewed life. This phenomenon lasted a few years.

I need to stress that my mother was very protective of me, and losing her instilled in me a never-ending feeling of imminent danger. I must admit that I experienced this feeling with different intensities for a long time—and this feeling passed when I met my wife, Pnina.

To this day, I do not know if that was a life necessity or a convenience on the part of my father, but he met a woman by the name of Rivka Royter. She was also a Polish refugee in Siberia who had left for Kyrgyzstan. He met her after returning from the Russian labor camp. She had a brother (Henry) who was mentally fragile and unable to survive on his own. They were both from a well-educated Jewish family originally from Warsaw. Her father was the owner of a drugstore and a highly recognized pharmacist.

Her parents, expecting a German invasion of Poland, sent both of them eastward to cross the Russian border illegally to flee the incoming Germans. This is how Rivka and Henry later became a part of my family. My father married Rivka in 1942, the year she became my stepmother. Sometime after their marriage, Rivka approached me and announced that she was my new mother. I strongly denied and resisted acknowledging this. I was bewildered about how a strange woman could declare she was my mother when my real mother had died recently. I violently and loudly denied her claim of being my mother for a fairly long time.

I cannot pinpoint the exact time when my conscience changed, and I started to recognize her as my newly adopted mother who was trying to help me in my daily life. She became very devoted to my well-being. I never went to bed hungry or thirsty. She always provided a doctor when I was ill. Back then, the doctors made house calls. She provided everything I needed to survive the ordeal in Kyrgyzstan.

Life in Kyrgyzstan was not easy, and the problems were compounded by a language barrier, strange habits, and a different culture. It was very hard getting used to eating while sitting on the floor or the habit of grabbing food with my fingers from a main plate while surrounded by others. Hygiene was not a consideration at all. Toiletry was scarce, and the facilities were located outside the dwelling unit. Then there was the frightening experience of watching the local population (Chechens) dancing with knives hanging in their mouths. This show was far from entertaining.

I started school around the age of seven. My stepmother made sure that I was properly prepared and well-dressed. She was overly concerned with making sure that I would do well in school. She was a graduate of the University of Warsaw, majoring in two languages, Esperanto and Latin.

My father was absent most of the time as he was trying to keep his business active. His main occupation was to acquire food and other domestic supplies at cheap prices and resell them for a profit. This method kept his business successful, and it kept my family alive.

One day, I came home from school to find my stepmother in tears. She was speaking to our neighbor, and the word *Treblinka* was mentioned several times. After a few days, I was told that her parents were deported from the Warsaw Ghetto to Treblinka, one of Hitler's killing centers. Her parents perished in a gas chamber. My stepmother was visibly devastated. It took me a while to understand the enormity of the disaster that befell Polish

Jews who did not run away from the invading Germans.

When I approached my father to get an explanation regarding the fate of my stepmother's parents, he answered, "Probably God does not exist. Otherwise, he would not permit such atrocities against innocent Jews."

When I continued by asking my father about why the phrase "chosen people" was given to the Jewish people (who had no help during this disaster), he stated, "We were chosen to suffer."

German Jews were a tiny fraction of the general population, but they wielded a disproportionate amount of power in private and national enterprises. Their economic standing served as a source of envy by the general German population.

Jews served in the German army in numbers exceeding their ratio to the general population. Many of them were declared heroes of the *fatherland* while fighting in World War I. Many of them received Black Crosses, military awards for bravery on the battlefield.

All this did not stop Hitler from blaming the Jews for treason. Hitler accused the Jews of backstabbing, which he believed brought

Germany to its knees and the eventual loss of World War I.

Hitler repeatedly accused the Jews of being attracted to revolutionary movements during the beginning of the millennium. He falsely accused every Jew of participating in the Bolshevik Revolution throughout European countries. This was a virulent lie. The truth is that only a tiny fraction of Jews supported revolutionary movements. This accusation was the main source of the intensification of hatred toward the Jewish population.

The Bolshevik Revolution of 1917 eluded that a successful outcome would put an end to antisemitism and racial discrimination. Pogroms against Jews in Tsarist Russia were a frequent occurrence. Jews were killed in the streets, and their homes and possessions were plundered and confiscated by murderous mobs. Some Jews hoped that they would find freedom from oppression, and the end of antisemitism should the revolution prove successful.

An absolute minority of Russian Jews were very active in the Bolshevik revolutionary apparatus. This included the administration of gulag camps. One of the biggest ironies and tragedies was that the Jews became prisoners and oppressors in the gulags. Five million landowners in Ukraine were sent to gulags with their families. Almost all of them perished from starvation and disease in the Siberian wilderness. Those Ukrainians who did not own arable land were left in place and subsequently perished from famine caused by a complete lack of basic food supplies.

It is no wonder that when the German army invaded Ukraine in 1941, the Ukrainians greeted the German soldiers as liberators. The Ukrainians were convinced that Hitler would make Ukraine a free nation again. The Ukrainians were unaware that Hitler designated Ukraine as a future colony, designating it as "Lebensraum" (living space) for German settlers.

The most fertile land in the world is located in Ukraine. It became a magnet for colonialism and conquest by Nazism. The resettled German population intended to own the arable land, making the Ukrainians a peasant-slave cast.

The hate and hostility against the Jews intensified in Germany as the war progressed. Hitler discovered that there were approximately three million Jews dispersed in small towns called *shtetls* in the Russian territory. The shtetls were the result of prohibition against the Jews by czars. This prohibited the Jews to live in large cities and only permitted them to live in a *Pale of Settlement.*

As mentioned previously, following the German army units was a death squad known as the *Einsatzgruppen.* These were special extermination units designated to kill all Jews caught in the overtaken territories. These four groups were designated as A, B, C, and D. They were spread along the length of the front line. Their leaders were highly educated Germans from the best universities. Most of them attained PhD degrees.

When these groups reached Ukraine, they found themselves questioned by the local Ukrainians. These Ukrainians asked for permission to kill the Jews themselves. The German soldiers who agreed became specta- tors to the slaughter. The Ukrainians vented their historical anger and tried to settle their grudge against the Jewish participation in the Bolshevik Revolution. The Ukrainians did not forget the atrocities of the gulags, the dis- possession of land, and the subsequent famine that caused approximately five million landowners and their families to die.

The killing of approximately three million Jews by gunfire in the forests became time-consuming and mentally draining for many German soldiers. It was also too slow in the destruction of European Jewry. To improve and accelerate the destruction of Jews, killing centers were erected in Poland. Treblinka was one of the killing centers designated for the Jews from Warsaw and its vicinity.

We continued to live in Kyrgyzstan until 1946. The country was in complete isolation, and there were no signs of economic development under Stalin's rule after the 1917 revolution. The country was historically ruled by Turks, Mongols, Kalmyks, Manchus, and Uzbeks before becoming part of the Russian Empire. Life in Kyrgyzstan was very primitive, with many places lacking electricity, running water, and medical facilities. After the death of my mother, my father was arrested several times for illegally selling food supplies. He was drafted into the Russian army. After my father was drafted into the Red Army, I remained under the close scrutiny of my brother. His pedantic nature was imposed on me with all the repercussions of his convictions. According to my brother, my stepmother did not wield authority when it came to controlling my behavior.

My brother was extremely strict and unforgiving toward my mistakes. His modus operandi was to tell me what to do and not how to do it. This incomplete communication between us caused me a lot of grief and suffering. The excursions he took (which included me) to look for food caused me a lot of anxiety and fear. One source of food in Kyrgyzstan was the cornfields which were owned and managed by the local government and the Kolkhoz. Entry into these fields was officially prohibited for private citizens.

One day, while playing outside with my friend Kola, my brother showed up unexpectedly at home. He ran into the house, gasping for air—he was obviously racing home. When he regained his breath, he told me that he was chased by a mounted police officer who had spotted him emerging from a cornfield with a sack full of corn ears. He was able to outrun the horse and saved himself from the trouble of being arrested for stealing government property. This crime carried a long prison term. After the chase, my brother decided to use me as his private sentry. I was in charge of his safety during his illegal ventures into the cornfields.

In case a mounted police officer appeared, I was to follow a preapproved script in case I was interrogated. To pass my brother's scrutiny, he asked me what my answer would be should I be asked, "Did you see a man going into the cornfield?"

My spontaneous first answer was, "That man told me to tell you that he is not in the field." Such an answer from me was met with a few blows to the head from my brother.

The cornfields were guarded by mounted police who made rounds along the edges of the planted area. My brother entered the fields with a sack to harvest the corn ears. My responsibility was to stay outside the corn-field and whistle when the mounted police would approach so that my brother would know to stay inside the cornfield. As long as I didn't whistle, he knew that there was no danger, and he would be able to get out without being arrested. The cornstalks were much taller than a person, and they provided ample cover from being detected once inside.

Many times, my brother attempted to verify if I understood my assignment before disappearing into the cornfield. If my response was not verbatim as per his instructions, I was subjected to summary punishment via a blow to the head. I never had the opportunity to correct my mistake. It took a while to forgive all these transgressions that I suffered because it was my brother's fight for survival for my family.

It became clear to me that my tendency to please others for most of my adult life had developed in early childhood by traumatic events that were perpetuated by the care given to me by my brother. Having a deceased mother, a missing father, a helpless step-mother, and an overdemanding brother were factors that shaped my early character. My other assignments included picking up dry cow manure to heat our home. The manure burnt very easily, making the room warm quickly. Any mistake on my part was met with a carnal penalty at the hands of my brother. These penalties included being whipped with white birch twigs over open flesh. I still remember my stepmother screaming, "Not in the head" when some of the whips landed close to my face. The white birch tree, one of several national Russian symbols, became my symbol of bodily harm and injury.

My brother's behavior toward me is probably the main reason I became a *people pleaser*. I became preoccupied with other people's opinions of me. It also instilled in me a constant hunger to be accepted and appreciated by others. I believe that my sense of deep responsibility for all my responsibilities came from the same source. It also appears that my brother's attitude toward me became a reason for my low self-esteem and the constant desire to exceed all imposed duties. Throughout my entire childhood, I never received from him an acknowledgment of satisfactory performance for anything he imposed on me. His behavior instilled in me a feeling of inferiority which took some time to overcome in my adult life.

It became obvious to me later in life that the lack of parental presence, guidance, and praise was the cause of my desire to perform superlatively in all tasks. To this day, it remains a mystery to me as to how my father was released from the Russian army.

Most of my time in Kyrgyzstan was spent helping my brother bring food and heating supplies to our home. From my recollection, I attended my first school year in Kyrgyzstan. It was a school run by a Jewish charity. We left Kyrgyzstan for Poland in 1946.

BACK IN POLAND

The end of World War II brought me to the town of Dzierżoniów, which is located in southwestern Poland. This medieval town, first mentioned in 1258, was ruled by the Kingdom of Bohemia and later inherited by the Habsburg Monarchy of Austria in 1526.

In 1742, the town was renamed Reichenbach, and it became part of the Kingdom of Prussia and eventually of Prussian-led Germany in 1871. The city of Dzierżoniów was annexed to Poland in 1945, following the end of World War II.

The German inhabitants were expelled to Germany, and the town was resettled by Poles and Jews from eastern Poland who had been governed by the Soviet Union. The German inhabitants were given half an hour to pick up their personal belongings and leave. Their homes were fully furnished, and in some cases, warm food was still on the table.

We moved into a four-bedroom apartment which was completely furnished. We felt satisfied that what had been done to the Jews in Germany and other German-controlled countries had befallen the German population this time. It was small retribution for what was done to the Polish population. The new residents in town included a substantial number of Jews which survived the Holocaust and the Russian gulags.

There was an intent to establish a Jewish settlement in Dzierżoniów, but this never materialized. My father's brother, living in the USA, sent passports for us to emigrate. This included my stepmother, Rivka. She refused to emigrate, for this would have left her brother Henry in Poland. She was unwilling to abandon her only brother after the loss of her parents in the Holocaust. Her decision forced us to stay in Poland. Many Jews attempted to emigrate to the United States before and right after the outbreak of World War II, but they hit a stone wall made of refusals to allow immigration.

The anti-immigration sentiment in the postwar Depression era was very intense. The Roosevelt administration, despite preaching the importance of immigration to the USA, did everything to impede the flow of Jewish immigrants trying to flee Europe.

In 1942, there was ample evidence indicating the systemic slaughter of European Jews by Hitler. Individuals like Charles Lindberg and Henry Ford were open supporters of Hitler, giving him full recognition and moral support for the war against communist Russia. Henry Ford was even sending donations to Hitler because of his promise of destroying communism. Despite Jewish demonstrations and the efforts of Henry Morgenthau, the Treasury Secretary in Roosevelt's cabinet, no increase in Jewish immigration to the USA took place. The quota of Jews admitted remained the same and never increased, despite the ongoing extermination of European Jews.

The refusal of my stepmother to separate from her only brother stranded us in Poland.

The town of Dzierżoniów was filling up with the survivors of the Holocaust and resettled Poles who survived World War II. The town started having more Jewish institutions such as grammar schools, an orphanage, and a synagogue.

My first Passover was here. It was organized by the Jewish community with financial help from American Jewry. I was tremendously impressed with the long procedure for the Seder meal which included recitations from the Haggadah as well as songs and questions asked by children. I also experienced my first Day of Atonement, known as *Yom Kippur*. I was taken aback by the recitation of serious transgressions by the participants of this solemn holiday. What caught my attention was the *Ashamnu* prayer that included admissions of sins that, in my opinion, most Jews did not commit.

A part of these admissions was that everyone at the table "stole and slandered, caused others to sin with malicious intent, gave bad advice, deceived, caused friends grief, acted stiff-necked, and refused to admit that our suffering was caused by our sins, had gone astray, and led others astray."

I remarked to my father that such untrue admissions as a whole were creating a bad image for the Jewish community, as well as being used by antisemites to stereotype all Jews. My father responded that we are all responsible collectively for what a few committed; therefore, we all need to ask for forgiveness. I responded that antisemites did not see it that way and that all of us are being blamed for crimes committed by very few people.

Henry, my stepmother's brother, married a beautiful woman named Paula. Henry was a symbol of ugliness. Professionally, he was a teacher of the Polish language. He was phobic in nature and lost his temper easily. On many Sundays, we were called by Paula to render emotional help and pacify her irritated husband. His most frequent complaint was that Paula was trying to kill him by serving him overly heated chicken soup. I was aware of the possibility of killing people with bullets but never with chicken soup. Many Sundays were ruined by Henry's emotionally exhausting behavior. The ordeal with Henry continued for a long time.

After the resettlement to western Poland, my father decided to visit Suwałki, our old home, the store, and the surrounding areas. Suwałki was well-known for having a well-kept Jewish cemetery. After reaching Suwałki, he utilized a local driver to visit all the familiar sites. He did not recognize the cemetery once he arrived. Not one single tombstone was left. The only thing left was a grassy area surrounded by an iron fence. The tombstones were removed by the Germans and used to pave the roads. There was no sign of the grocery store or the house we owned. The store was robbed by the locals, and the land was confiscated by the Russian-installed communist Polish government.

There was no Jewish survivor in Suwałki. Today, Suwałki does not have any Jewish residents. There are no other remnants of Jewish existence there.

DEPARTING POLAND

The eruption of World War II caught Poland with the largest Jewish population in Europe. There were approximately 3.3 million Jews in prewar Poland. Since medieval times, Jews were forbidden from owning land and were not allowed to be farmers or to join any craftsman's guilds. Jews became traders, a profession which handled money.

This type of occupation allowed Polish kings to issue open invitations for Jews to settle in Poland. Ironically, in Hebrew, Poland is pronounced *Polania*, which stands for "here I live." Poland became the *promised land* for all European Jews for more than five hundred years.

Their affinity for money management made the Jews the most important tool in the collection of taxes for the Polish kings. Jews became the darlings of the Polish kings, and they were hated among the Polish peasants. Prosperity and personal security for Polish Jews were established around the fifteenth century in Poland. The expulsion of Jews from other countries brought waves of Jewish refugees to Poland.

The largest population of Jews in Poland became a historical paradox, despite rampant antisemitism in prewar Poland. The reign of King Zygmunt, the Protector of Jews, brought a strong policy of support toward Jews, granting autonomous community life.

On July 4, 1946, Poland welcomed the returning Jewish Holocaust and gulag survivors with a Kielce pogrom which killed about forty Jews and wounding many others. This bloodbath was triggered by the disappearance of a Polish boy who went to visit his friend without his parents' permission or knowledge.

The rumor was that the boy was killed by Jews to use his blood for baking matzah, a traditional Jewish staple eaten during Passover. The boy returned from his unapproved visit to his friend's house alive and well. This blood libel was resurrected again to justify murdering the surviving Jews in Kielce in postwar Poland.

I remember my stepmother becoming very distraught and frightened. She kept asking my father how such a catastrophic killing like this pogrom could happen after the loss of six million Jews. She continued to question if there was not enough blood spilled in the Poland killing centers such as Treblinka, Chelmno, Sobibor, and Auschwitz.

The Kelce pogrom brought a serious consideration for us—whether to stay or leave Poland. It also brought about the question of Jewish self-defense during antisemitic onslaughts which caused personal harm and the loss of Jewish life. Most importantly, the question of owning arms for personal protection became a key consideration. My father stressed many times that owning arms would provide some level of protection for Jewish life.

Presently, while writing this memoir, my family resides in the USA, a blessed country with the right to bear arms. Throughout history, the right to bear arms for Jewish people was made impossible. When Hitler came to power, he forbade all Jews from owning firearms. The penalty for noncompliance was death. The prohibition of owning arms was enacted by the communist regime in Poland after the war.

The same thing happened in Tzarist Russia, leaving the Jews defenseless during the never-ending pogroms. The same regime that forbade Jews from owning arms is the same one that required twenty-five years of military service forced upon all Jews via a draft. A similar situation occurred in Turkey. This resulted in the loss of life of millions of defenseless Armenians.

Attached to my bedroom in Dzierżoniów was a commercial space that was used as a store by the former owner of our apartment. The commercial area was not in use when we were given the apartment. After some time, my father rented this area to three Jewish brothers, all survivors of the Holocaust. The brothers turned it into a butcher shop, where they sold various meats and other goods. One night, we were awoken by the Polish police and advised to stay away from my bedroom. After many questions, we were told that the brothers were killed in the store, execution style.

My father and stepmother were in deep shock and disbelief. They decided to leave Poland for good. In preparing to leave Poland, my father started selling our meager possessions in an open-air market. Saving for a rainy day was my father's second religion. As a child with no living parents, my father never knew when his next meal would be available. Saving money became a life necessity.

Only my father and my brother knew about the foreign currency savings which were hidden in empty and buried beer bottles in the small inner patio of our apartment. I clearly remember them returning with these bottles after the decision to depart Poland was made. Their faces became ash-like in color when the bottles were retrieved and opened. The savings, made in American dollars, was totally destroyed because of water that penetrated the defective corks. Instead of crisp bank notes, black powder poured out of the bottles.

This was the second time that my father lost his life savings. The first was the confiscation of his savings by the secret police in the gulag. Penniless again, my father made the decision to leave Poland for a second time.

My stepsister, Gustava, was born in 1948. Her birth changed my life dramatically. Having a predilection for catching colds, she was often ill until the age of seven. I found myself standing in line after school to retrieve her medication instead of going home to complete my studies. Her physician (Dr. Hollinger), a survivor of the Holocaust, was an almost-daily guest in our home. She was beautiful, extremely bright, and quite talented.

The worsening economic condition in postwar Poland brought on the fear of additional pogroms in Poland. To avoid a repeat of the Kielce pogrom, the Polish-installed Russian government chose to open free emigration for the surviving Jews. My family, including my married brother and his adopted daughter, emigrated to Israel. My stepmother's brother chose to emigrate to Denmark, a country that was historically friendly to Jews.

To get the attention of Steven Spielberg (to create a movie documenting the trials and tribulations that befell the eight hundred thousand Polish and Jewish people who were incarcerated in gulags during World War II by the Soviet regime) remains a humble wish. The survival rate in the gulags because of cold, malnutrition, lack of sanitation, and lice and typhoid was approximately 10 percent. This documentary would also include the slaughter of Polish officers who were taken as prisoners by the invading Russian army in Katyn. In the spring of 1940, they were massacred by the NKVD (Russian secret police) and later discovered in mass graves by invading Germans. The slaughter included twenty-two thousand Polish military officers and other highly educated residents who held government posts in prewar Poland.

EPILOGUE

About two thousand years ago, the Jewish people were given a choice—abandon their religion and convert to another or disappear from sight. The Jews chose none of the above. The refusal to comply with these demands brought about long-lasting penalties which included exclusion from many places in the world, and the Jews became permanent objects of draconian laws.

Jews were prohibited from entering certain professions and from owning land. The few permissible trades were traders, tailors, and shoemakers. Ecumenical laws from the Middle Ages and a repeated version in the form of the Nuremberg Laws in the 1930s (enacted by Hitler) locked the German Jews out of most professions and from holding government positions.

Jews were required to carry badges as a different caste of people. The same procedure was repeated by the Nazis in the 1930s when the Jews were required to wear a yellow Star of David. These imposed limitations forced a minor part of the Jewish population to join political movements that were historically doomed for failure.

A popular saying was eventually coined about the Jews. It stated that the problems and the suffering of the Jews were caused by the Jewish need to serve the wrong masters, to relieve the hardships imposed on them. An example of this claim includes serving the Polish kings at the expense of poor Polish peasants who had to pay taxes to the king, taxes collected by Jewish tax collectors.

Another example was the Jewish participation in the Bolshevik Revolutions in Russia and other European countries. A minority of Jewish communist sympathizers and activists bore the blame for the loss of five million Ukrainian landowners and fifteen million Russians.

The fatal attraction of Jews to revolutionary movements which promised social and religious freedoms caused tragic results perpetrated by Jew haters, including Hitler. Adolf Hitler, the archenemy of the Jewish people, used the participation of a few Jews in revolutionary movements as a justification for the annihilation of all Jews in Europe.

The fact that communism was totally void of religion did not preclude the Jews from participating in and supporting it. To this day, some Jews try to act as the moral compass of the world. Paradoxically, the Jewish endeavor to better the world for mankind has ultimately brought more hatred upon them.

Of the 3.3 million Jews in Poland, only 380,000 remained after the end of World War II. One of the ironies discovered in postwar Poland was the lack of Jewish culture which became the de facto Polish culture throughout the millennia. To restore this void, many native Poles enrolled in universities to learn the Yiddish language to be able to return Jewish song, dance, and theater to the Polish stage.

This effort was undertaken despite rampant antisemitism which was supported by the Communist postwar government.

The Holocaust caused not only physical destruction but also permanent intellectual damage to all mankind. This immeasurable loss to humanity does not have definite borders. This includes incalculable losses in the fields of philosophy, research, acting, writing, medicine, and an unknown number of lost Nobel laureates.

One and a half million Jewish children perished in the Holocaust. I could have been one of them. The reason given by the Nazis during the Nuremberg Trials was to destroy the future generation of avengers for what befell the Jewish people.

This is the main reason I wrote this memoir.